Soul Sex

The Ultimate Pleasure

Andrew Lawrence

Name   : Soul Sex: The Ultimate Pleasure

ISBN   : 1450522882

EAN-13   : 9781450522885

Color   : B/W with No Bleed

Country of
Publication   : United States

Author   : Andrew Lawrence

Cover Design: Andrew Lawrence

Book Format : Wicked Sunny (www.Publishinggurus.com)

Books by Andrew Lawrence

Soul Sex: The Ultimate Pleasure
How To Thrive After 65
Glimmers Of Hope
The Happiness Transformation
MONEY - The Basics
Discover Your Life Purpose in 30 minutes
Stories Of A Lifetime

About the book

Yes, the author could have written a 500-page book about the soul, and sex. But, in today's busy fast-paced world, nobody wants to read through 500 pages about **anything**. So, with that in mind, this is a short book. Short and to the point. Short, to the point, very interesting and very enlightening.

It takes your soul - and your sex life - to a whole new level.

TABLE OF CONTENTS

Introduction

Before we get to the soul sex there's a few things you should know ...

For the purposes of this book the spirit is the same as the soul. Soul Sex: the ultimate pleasure is a book about the soul. Your soul. And sex.

Yes, I know, a book about the soul, and soul sex, is controversial. The devoutly religious won't like it because they'll think it's not totally based on religion and the non-religious won't like it because they'll think it's totally based on religion. Well, it's both. And it's neither. This book is a combination of research, religious and non-religious spirituality - and years figuring out what the soul is, what it does, why it exists. And, of course, discovering soul sex.

The book was written with two purposes in mind. Firstly, to inspire, to motivate, to enlighten, to help people to be more in touch with their soul and to stay in touch with their soul. This is not an easy task in today's busy, fast-paced technologically driven world. The second purpose is to take sex to a whole new level. Hopefully, the book accomplishes both.

Andrew Lawrence
Los Angeles, California

Part 1 Spirituality

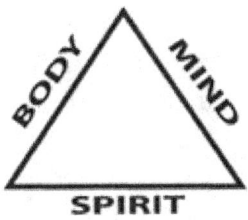

Spirituality and sex. A weird combination? Hardly. The human race has been combining spirituality and sex for thousands of years. Just not in the same way that Soul Sex combines them. In this book you will find interesting and enlightening things about spirituality, both religious and non-religious, in this book you will find interesting and enlightening things about the soul and in this book you will find **very** interesting and **very** enlightening things about sex. This book combines all these and culminates in something extremely interesting and extremely enlightening, something that I call soul sex. First, here are some interesting and enlightening things about religion and spirituality ...

History shows that religion and spirituality started a long long time ago; way before modern civilization, way before Judaism and Christianity, way before humans believed in one God. In the beginning, religion was based on nature ...

In the beginning, non-biblically, there was fear and superstition. Fear of darkness, fear of thunder, fear of lightning, fire, floods, drought, earthquakes, volcanoes and other natural phenomena. These natural occurrences were not understood and their causes were attributed to various gods. This led to early man offering sacrifices to appease the various gods, to avoid death and destruction and to bring good luck. In ancient times, prior to 2,000 BC, people believed in many gods, mainly gods relating to the earth, the heavens, the planting and harvesting of crops, and fertility. Many if not most of the ancient civilizations all had many gods.

Ancient mythological gods and goddesses include:

Thor   Norse god of thunder

Ra   Egyptian sun god

Zeus   Greek king of the gods and the god of the sky and thunder

Poseidon Greek god of the sea. God of earthquakes as well

Aphrodite Greek goddess of love, lust, beauty

Cupid   Roman god of Love

Venus   Roman goddess of love and beauty

Apollo   Roman god of the sun

Lakshmi   Hindu Goddes of Prosperity

The belief in only one God started with Abraham, around 2,000 BC, and eventually was adopted by other religions.

Timeline of major organized religions:

2,000 BC - Judaism (Abraham)
1,500 BC - Hinduism
560 BC - Buddhism
550 BC -Taoism
30 AD - Christianity
600 AD - Islam

Religious intolerance

Throughout the ages, in the name of God, and the salvation of the soul, much murder and mayhem has been committed. Some religions had many religious offenses that were punishable by death. One of the most infamous religious groups was the *Inquisition*, which was formed in order to maintain and regulate Catholic Orthodoxy under the Spanish monarchy. The Inquisition was formed in 1478, and for nearly 400 years they tortured and executed hundreds and thousands of Jews, Muslims and even other Christians across Europe, in the name of religion.

In human history, people have been put to death for religious crimes in almost every conceivable way. Some of the more widely used methods have been:

Crucifixion
Drowning
Buried alive
Beaten to death
Impaled
Stoning

Hanging

Beheading

Being thrown from a large rock

Pressing (having heavy weights placed on one's chest)

Being boiled alive

Burnt at the stake

On the other hand, over the past 2,000-4,000 years, religion has also provided billions of people with a positive life structure, a moral code to live by, and something to believe in.

Today, Over 80% of Americans believe in God. Billions of people all over the world believe in God, under one name or another, depending on their religion. A Supreme Being. An Unknowable Entity. Creator of the universe. Billions of people all over the world pray to God. Some pray to God nightly before they go to bed, some pray to God on Sunday or Saturday, some pray to God five times a day.

Others do not believe in God. Still others believe in science or the laws of the universe or mysticism or spiritualism or paganism or believe in nothing at all. Some believe in a combination of God and the spiritual universe, betting both sides.

Whether you believe in God or not, the reality is that you can't prove, or disprove, that God exists. Does God exist? This is one of the oldest questions, one of the oldest mysteries, in human existence. This mystery may never be solved. It's a matter of faith, not fact. In the meantime we live our lives, according to our beliefs. In

the meantime we do the best we can. In the meantime we
get caught up in our daily lives; places to go, people to
see, things to do, mouths to feed. In the meantime we are
born, we live, we grow old, we die. And we have sex.

In human history, going back thousands of years, God
and sex go hand in hand. Did ancient cultures and early
civilizations have gods and goddesses of sex? Yes.
Ancient cultures and early civilizations that honored gods
and goddesses of sex include ...

Greek
Roman
Egyptian
Hindu/India
Chinese
Japanese
African
Mayan
Norse
Celtic

Quotes about God ...

When questioning the actions of God we always were told by religious leaders (and often our parents) that "God works in mysterious ways". And that, as mere mortals, we are not capable of understanding those mysterious ways. That being the case, since there are no good answers to the question of why God does what He does, perhaps it's a good idea to also have a sense of humor about it. If so, here are some thought provoking, and humorous, quotes about You Know Who ...

"When you want something really bad and you close your eyes and wish for it-- God's the guy who ignores you."

> - Caspian Tredwell-Owen, and
> Alex Kurtzman, *The Island, 2005*

"What can you say about a society that says that God is dead and Elvis is alive?"

> - Irv Kupcinet

"If only God would give me some clear sign! Like making a large deposit in my name in a Swiss bank."

> - Woody Allen

"Is there a God? I hope so. Because when I die, hopefully I will meet God and, when I do meet God, I have a lot of questions for Him!"

> - Andrew Lawrence

"In Genesis, it says that God created the world in six days and on the seventh day He rested. He rested? That implies that He was tired. He's God, the Almighty, the All Powerful, how can He be tired? Plus, He took the entire 7th day off. I would think that, being God, if He was tired a short nap would have been enough."

- Andrew Lawrence

"If you say you speak to God that's considered normal. If you say that God speaks to you that's considered insanity."

- Andrew Lawrence

"God gave man two heads; a little head and a big head, with no control over either one."

- Andrew Lawrence

"The way God designed it, as you age you gain wisdom. Unfortunately, by the time you acquire wisdom you'll be too old to use it."

- Andrew Lawrence

"From 'dust to dust' is a poetic way to describe the life cycle. In reality, it's more like 'from diapers to diapers'."

- Andrew Lawrence

"God gave Moses ten commandments. Since then life has become a lot more complicated, with a lot more ways to sin and only ten commandments to live by. I think we need at least another ten."

- Andrew Lawrence

Part 2 The soul

We are made up of 3 overall major systems; the Body, the Mind and the Spirit.

The Body

The human body is made up of 206 bones and more than 650 muscles, plus tendons and other assorted things which hold the body together and allow it to move. According to the U.S. Geological Survey, "up to 60 percent of the human body is water, the brain is composed of 70 percent water, and the lungs are nearly 90 percent water. About 83 percent of our blood is water." Bodies come in all shapes and sizes. In the end, the body is highly bio-degradable, except for the larger bones.

Besides housing the systems and physically supporting the systems for movement, another function of the body is reproduction. Reproduction of the species. Reproduction is a built-in natural biological function in all species. And, biologically, to aid and heighten the reproductive desire in Man, God created women with breasts. This biological reproductive desire is the main reason why so many men go wild over large hooters.

The Mind

The mind, especially the brain, runs the body. The mind
tells the body what to do, interprets feelings such as
pleasure, pain, sadness, happiness, anger, etc, interprets
the five senses of sight, sound, smell, touch and taste.
Much is known about the brain but, considering the
complexity of this organ, only a fraction has been learned
about how and why the brain works the way it does.
Basically, the brain is an electro-chemical system of
neurons. Neurons are cells that send signals to and from
the brain and nervous system. There are approximately
100 billion neurons in the brain. The mind also performs
other functions such as thinking, deciding what to eat
for dinner, remembering your user name and password,
dreaming up ridiculous excuses when you get stopped by
a cop for speeding, and overriding your emotions to keep
you out of trouble. It's also the little voice in your head
that tells you what's right and wrong; the little voice to
which we often decide not to listen.

The Spirit

The body houses our systems. The mind runs the body.
No one knows what the spirit does. Much is known about
the body. Much is known about the mind. Almost nothing
is known about the spirit, the soul. The soul is a mystery.
The soul is a mystery, even after thousands of years of
scientific, philosophical and religious study. Yet the soul
is an integral part of us. Each of has a soul. All of us have
a soul.

The soul connects us to the universe. The soul connects
us to each other. The soul gives us the ability to be more
than just a body and a brain. The soul gives us the ability

to rise above the adversities of life, to do good and great works, to appreciate nature and harmony and beauty. The soul allows us to recognize each other on a different spiritual level, an ancient primitive level, and to be part of the whole, to be at one with the universe. To be at one with God.

What is the soul made of?
The soul remains mostly a mystery. Scientifically, we do not know what it is made of or where it resides within us or how it's physically connected to us. What is the soul made of? Nobody knows. It's not animal, mineral or vegetable. It's not a solid, a liquid or a gas. It's something else and nobody knows what the something else is. Scientists cannot see it, feel it, hear it, smell it, touch it, taste it or measure it, or prove it exists. It cannot be categorized. It cannot be classified. What is it made of? We don't know. Perhaps some form of energy, material unique unto itself, some sort of universal material or energy we simply do not understand. Whatever the soul is made of has never been satisfactorily explained by science, religion, philosophy or psychology, It is an unknown. Elusive and unknown, even after thousands, or perhaps even millions, of years. A mystery? Yes. One of life's oldest and greatest mysteries? Yes.

To paraphrase the poet Robert Browning ...
"I have written 3 books about the soul, and still know little or nothing about it."

The soul exists. It is part of the universe. Each of us has a soul ... made of the same substance ... and our soul is somehow connected to us and connected to all other souls.

How is the soul connected to us?
We do not know how the soul is connected to our body and mind. We do not know how souls are connected to other souls. Your body is yours. Your mind is yours. Your soul is not yours, it belongs to God (or, if you prefer, the universe) and is returnable upon death.

How does the soul operate?
After thousands and thousands of years we know little or nothing about the physical properties of the soul. That is because the soul is not a physical thing and does not have physical properties. The soul is part of the spiritual realm, the metaphysical universe. As such, the soul operates according to its own rules, different rules, not the rules of science, not the rules of law, not the rules of Man.

Why do we have a soul?
No one knows for sure. Theologians and philosophers might claim that we have a soul because God gives each of us a part of Him. To use for a lifetime. Physicians might claim that they don't know anything about it medically and, therefore, don't treat the soul. Scientists might claim that they cannot measure the soul or recreate it in the lab so they often dismiss the soul as unscientific. And many individuals are non-spiritual or un-enlightened and might even deny they have a soul. Everyone has a soul. Yes, YOU have a soul.

We have a soul because we are a special part of the universe and the soul is part of the energy of the universe.

What your soul wants

The soul, your soul, does not want money, a new car, new clothes, new shoes or a new handbag. Your soul does not want to be petty, vengeful, angry, sad, confused, tired or sick. Your soul does not want obesity or anorexia, more TV or more text messages. Your soul does not need a college education or a PhD or a better job or a hot stock or more credit cards. Your soul does not want to drink beer or wine or scotch or rum or bourbon or gin or vodka. Your soul does not want to snort cocaine, shoot heroin, do methamphetamines or smoke marijuana. Your soul does not want to smoke cigars or cigarettes. Your soul does not want to pig out on tons of cheeseburgers, pizza, ice cream, potato chips or chocolate (though a little chocolate IS good for the soul).

The soul wants few things. The things a soul wants do not cost money. The things the soul wants are free. It wants Peace. It wants Love. It wants Nature. It wants Beauty. It wants to be Recognized. It wants Bliss. It wants to be Happy.

All souls are equal

It doesn't matter if you live in Europe, Asia, Africa, North America, South America or Australia - you have a soul. It doesn't matter if you're Caucasian, black, Asian, Indian, Hispanic, Native American, Samoan, Eskimo or other nationality or race - you have a soul. It doesn't matter if you're a billionaire, a millionaire, or broke - you have a soul. It doesn't matter if you live in a big mansion or a cardboard box - you have a soul. It doesn't matter if you live in a big city or a tiny village - you have a soul.

It doesn't matter if you have multiple PhD's or you're a high school dropout - you have a soul. It doesn't matter who you work for or what you do for a living - you have a soul. It doesn't matter if you're male, female or both - you have a soul. Everyone, each of us, has a soul. And all souls are equal.

All souls are equal and all souls are pure and "good". Regardless of bad (or evil) behavior the essence, the soul, of a person is "good". The problem is that many people are not in touch with this part of themselves, not in touch with their soul, and commit bad acts, acts that harm others, ignoring or overriding their soul.

Like the mind, it takes years for us to develop and integrate the soul. Children are basically unaware of their soul and remain so, usually until their late teens/early 20's. And, lest we forget, many adults remain blissfully unaware of their soul throughout their entire lifetime. That's part of spiritual development and spiritual evolution.

In broad terms the stages of spiritual development are:

Dormant
Awakening
Seeking
Attaining
Advancing
Mastery

Dormant

The soul is not awake. The person may not realize (or may deny) that they have a soul. The dormant soul person is not spiritually developed though they may be highly intelligent. Often, the dormant soul person is not interested in spiritual development and often wants proof that the soul even exists.

Awake

The soul is not dormant and is somewhat integrated with the mind and body. The person realizes that they have a soul and that they are at the beginning stages of spiritual development. The awake soul person may or may not be interested in seeking further enlightenment.

Aware

The soul is awake and functioning and more integrated with the mind and body. The person realizes they have a soul and is in the first real stage of spiritual development. The aware soul person is often open to further enlightenment.

Seeking

The seeker is aware of his or her soul and the soul is more integrated with the mind and body. The seeking person is actively interested in further spiritual development and often reads a large number of self-help and spiritually oriented books seeking to further his or her knowledge and understanding of spiritual matters.

Attaining

The attaining person is in touch with his soul and its integration with the mind and body. This person is in the mid-to-upper ranges of spiritual development and is becoming more and more enlightened. The attaining person is more selective in his reading and has a lot of spiritual knowledge and a clearer understanding of his or her enlightenment.

Advancing

The advancing person is well aware of their soul and the soul is well integrated with the mind and body. The advancing person is able to further his or her own spiritual development and enlightenment on their own and understands their place in the universe and their purpose in life. They are at the higher stages of spiritual development.

Master

The master is fully aware of their soul and has complete integration of soul, mind and body. The functioning of the soul is equal to, or greater than, the functioning of the mind and body. The master needs no further spiritual knowledge and is at the highest level of spiritual development and enlightenment. Masters are rare. And, should you come across one, they have the answers you seek.

Everyone is at a different stage of spiritual development. And everyone develops (or doesn't develop) at their own pace. For those who seek, it is a lifelong quest … until you realize there is nothing to seek. Until you realize that everything is as it is supposed to be, and you accept it all and, as a result, you find the deep peace and bliss that comes from being connected to, being a part of, everything.

I know, it's a lot to absorb and for many readers all this is a bit dense and a bit deep. You may want to reread this part of the book numerous times as you progress through your own spiritual development stages; you will understand more each time you read it.

What makes the soul happy?

The soul retreats from chaos, noise, confusion and
negativity. The soul wants peace not war, the soul wants
harmony not disorder, the soul wants love not hate, the
soul wants happiness not sadness. Your soul wants to be
fulfilled not deprived.

What does the soul want?
• Nature
• Beauty
• Harmony
• Recognition
• Love

Your soul longs for Beauty. Your soul longs for Nature.
Your soul longs for Recognition. Your soul longs for
recognition from other souls. Did you ever meet someone
for the first time and feel like you knew that person for a
long time? That's the recognition of someone's soul.

The soul smile
When strangers smile or nod at you, without speaking,
that's their soul recognizing your soul. Saying hello. I
often smile or nod at perfect strangers and rarely fail to
get a nod or smile in return. That is my soul recognizing
their soul and their soul returning the greeting. It feels
good. It's good for the soul. It makes the soul happy.
That recognition connects souls, connects people at a
higher level, a spiritual level, a metaphysical level, the
level of the soul. And also makes you feel that you are
not alone.

The soul smile may be just a small smile and that's OK, as long as the soul smile is **genuine.** Put a smile on your face. And in your soul. When you give a stranger a simple genuine little soul smile it will make them happy … and will make YOU happy! Try it and see.

Soul moods

Your soul has its own moods. The soul can be happy,
sad, depressed, elated, deprived, fulfilled, dormant or
awake. The moods of the soul are dependent on whether
or not you are giving the soul what it wants. The mood
of the soul affects your body and your mind. The moods
of the soul are often difficult to tell from the emotions
and moods of the mind. If you do not have enough
money, you may become unhappy and depressed. That's
the mind deciding to be depressed or unhappy. If you
feel isolated or lonely that could be either the mood
of the mind or the mood of the soul, or both. A good
way to tell if it's a mind mood is to ask yourself what
would make you feel better. If the answer is something
material, something physical or emotional, i.e. money,
a new car, more love, it's probably a mind mood. If the
answer is something non-material, something spiritual,
it's probably a soul mood. If you don't know what's
causing a strong, long lasting mood that doesn't make
you happy or interferes with your enjoyment of life, it's
probably time to change your life, and/or see a doctor or
a therapist.

Take a soul break
It's very important to take time out from your busy
schedule and just quietly be with yourself ... and just
quietly be with your soul. Take a soul break. Do it
regularly. Try to do it every day or several times a day.
As little as 5 minutes in a quiet place with no distractions
helps to clear your mind and renew your spirit. Make
time. It can really help you a lot, especially if you have
a lot of stress in your life. Just a few deep breaths, or a

short walk, can make a big difference in your outlook, your energy, your focus, and your ability to cope. Take a break! Take a 5-minute soul break from your work, your spouse, your family, your kids, your problems, your self. It's one of the single best things you can do. It's simple, it's quick and it's free! Take a soul break! The benefits to your mind, your body and your soul can be enormous!

Take a soul break and get in touch with some nature, some beauty ... and nourish your soul.

Immortality

Souls are immortal. Humans are not. Your soul is immortal. You are not.

The soul is "on loan" from God (or, if you prefer, the universe). The soul is on loan from God (or the universe) to be kept and used by the individual for their lifetime and, upon death, to be returned from whence it came.

Why are we given a soul?

No one knows for sure. No one knows for sure why we are given a soul; not scientists, not religious leaders, not psychologists, not teachers, not spiritual leaders, not philosophers, not the government. No one knows for sure why we have a soul.

There are a lot of theories about why we have a soul but no proof. There are two major theories about why we have a soul. One theory is religious, the other is metaphysical/spiritual.

The religious theory holds that we are created in God's image and, as such, we are given a part of Him - a soul - in order to maintain, over our lifetime, a special, unique connection with the Creator. The soul is God's gift to us. To each of us. Upon death, the soul departs the body and returns to God.

The metaphysical/spiritual theory is that we are all, each of us, part of the universe. And all of us, each of us, have the same unique and universal material - the soul - which connects us to everything, and everyone. Upon death, the soul departs the body and returns to the universe.

In both theories that material - the soul - does not die. It's immortal.

Your soul is a special gift, wherever it came from.
Your soul is a special wondrous part of you. A special wondrous immortal part of you. A special wondrous immortal part of you that is yours for your entire lifetime. It would be a shame to ignore it. Or disrespect it. Or not feed it.

Part 3 Sex

And now it's time for sex!

There is a reason we want sex. It's a natural, often strong, biological desire and need. Sex can also be an expression of love. Plus, sex feels good. Really good. And it can be fun. Really fun.

I assume you are interested in sex (if you weren't interested in sex you wouldn't be reading this book). Thousands of books have been written on the subject of sex, thousands of paintings have been painted depicting sex, millions of people will have, or have had, relationships based on sex. We think about sex. We fantasize about sex. We experiment with sex. Today, sex is everywhere; on TV, in the movies, in books, in magazines and on the internet. We have sex everywhere; in a bed, in a chair, on the floor, on the kitchen table, on the dining room table, on the conference room table, in a car, in an elevator, outdoors, at home, at work, in the morning, in the afternoon and at night. We are sexual beings. Sex is part of life. Sex even effects our health.

What are the health benefits of sex?

Your Health. Is Sex Necessary?
by Alan Farnham, Forbes Magazine

"Fans of abstinence had better be sitting down … the best that modern science can say for sexual abstinence is that it's harmless when practiced in moderation. Having regular and enthusiastic sex, by contrast, confers a host of measurable physiological advantages, be you male or female. (This assumes that you are engaging in sex without contracting a sexually transmitted disease.)

In one of the most credible studies correlating overall health with sexual frequency, Queens University in Belfast tracked the mortality of about 1,000 middle-aged men over the course of a decade. The study was designed to compare persons of comparable circumstances, age and health. Its findings, published ... in the *British Medical Journal*, were that men who reported the highest frequency of orgasm enjoyed a death rate half that of the laggards. Other studies ... purport to show that having sex even a few times a week has an associative or causal relationship with the following:

- **Improved sense of smell:** After sex, production of the hormone prolactin surges. This in turn causes stem cells in the brain to develop new neurons in the brain's olfactory bulb, its smell center.

- **Reduced risk of heart disease:** In a 2001 follow-on to the Queens University study mentioned above, researchers focused on cardiovascular health. Their finding? That by having sex three or more times a week, men reduced their risk of heart attack or stroke by half.

- **Weight loss, overall fitness:** Sex, if nothing else, is exercise. A vigorous bout burns some 200 calories-- about the same as running 15 minutes on a treadmill .... The pulse rate, in a person aroused, rises from about 70 beats per minute to 150, the same as that of an athlete putting forth maximum effort. British researchers have determined that the equivalent of six Big Macs can be worked off by having sex three times a week for a year. Muscular contractions during intercourse work the pelvis, thighs, buttocks, arms, neck and thorax. Sex also boosts production of testosterone, which leads to stronger bones and muscles. *Men's Health* magazine has gone so far as to call the bed the single greatest piece of exercise equipment ever invented.

- **Pain-relief:** Immediately before orgasm, levels of the hormone oxytocin surge to five times their normal level. This in turn releases endorphins, which alleviate the pain of everything from headache to arthritis to even migraine. In women, sex also prompts production of estrogen, which can reduce the pain of PMS.

- **Less-frequent colds and flu:** Wilkes University in Pennsylvania says individuals who have sex once or twice a week show 30% higher levels of an antibody called immunoglobulin A, which is known to boost the immune system.

- **Better bladder control:** Heard of Kegel exercises? You do them, whether you know it or not, every time you stem your flow of urine. The same set of muscles is worked during sex.

- **Better teeth:** Seminal plasma contains zinc, calcium and other minerals shown to retard tooth decay. Thus oral sex performed on a man could be a far richer, more complex and more satisfying dental experience than squeezing a tube of Crest. Researchers have noted, in addition, that sexual etiquette usually demands the brushing of one's teeth before and/or after intimacy, which, by itself, would help promote better oral hygiene.

While possession of a robust appetite for sex--and the physical ability to gratify it--may not always be the formula for perfect health, a reluctance to engage can be a sign that something is seriously on the fritz, especially where the culprit is an infirm erection.

Dr. J. Francois Eid, a urologist with Weill Medical College of Cornell University and New York Presbyterian Hospital, observes that erectile dysfunction is an extension of the vascular system. A lethargic penis may be telling you that you have diseased blood vessels elsewhere in your body. "It could be a first sign of hypertension or diabetes or increased cholesterol levels. It's a red flag that you should see your doctor." Treatment and exercise, says Dr. Eid, can have things looking up again: "Men who exercise and have a good heart and low heart rate, and who are cardio-fit, have firmer erections. There very definitely is a relationship."

But is there such a thing as too *much* sex?

The answer, in purely physiological terms, is this: If you're female, probably not. If you're male? You betcha.

Dr. **Claire Bailey** of the University of Bristol says there is little or no risk of a woman's overdosing on sex. In fact, she says, regular sessions can not only firm a woman's tummy and buttocks but also improve her posture."

Sex facts

And from RandomHistory.com here are some interesting facts about sex …

On average, adult men think about sex every seven seconds.

Having sex at least once per week can lower a man's risk of heart disease by 30%, stroke by 50%, and diabetes by 40%. It has also been shown that men with an active sex life are more likely to live past 80 years.

The average size of an erect penis measures between 5 and 6 inches, while the average size of a flaccid penis is about 3.5 inches.

Use of the condom was first noted in published literature in the early 1500s. The device was originally made of linen, and historians believe the legendary lover Casanova used linen condoms.

Historical records show that even in 1850 B.C., women attempted to practice birth control. The most common method was a mixture of crocodile dung and honey placed in the vagina in the hopes of preventing pregnancy.

Although nearly any body part or item of clothing may be an object of sexual fetishism, the shoe and the foot are the two most common fetishes in Western society.

Just a decade ago, only 25% of women reported

experiencing orgasm as a result of intercourse. In recent years, this number has risen to about 45%. In contrast, over 80% of women report experiencing orgasm though oral sex.

Throughout the United States, approximately 4% of the population self-identifies as gay, lesbian, or bisexual.

Approximately 1% of people worldwide identify as asexual (having no strong sexual attraction to either sex).

Statistics suggest that approximately one in every five Americans has indulged in sex with a colleague at work.

Approximately 70% of people in the U.S. admit to fantasizing about group sex at some point in their life, and more than 50% of those people actually follow through.

Statistics show that approximately 90% of men and 65% of women masturbate from time to time.

Worldwide, 27.5% of women report that they felt pressured into having sex for the first time compared to 15% of men reporting the same feelings.

According to a 2007 worldwide sex survey, the average age when people first have sex is 19.25. The survey also found that people in Asian countries tended to lose their virginity at a much later age (an average of 22) than those in Western cultures (an average of 18).

Outside of the bedroom, the most common place for

adults in the U.S. to have sex is the car.

The average couple spends about 20 minutes engaged in sexual foreplay prior to intercourse.

Worldwide, sexually active adults report having sex an average of 103 times per year. This number is down from an average of 127 times per year in 2003.

One report states that 48% of women have faked an orgasm at least once in their life. Interestingly, an identical 48% of men also report faking an orgasm at least once.

Throughout the world, approximately 25% of people report having had only one sexual partner. Conversely, 21% of people report having more than 10 sexual partners in their lifetime.

One survey reports that 53% of sexually active Americans claim to have sex at least once weekly.

Only 48% of Americans report being satisfied with their sex life.

Many of the ingredients in chocolate are proven to cause arousal similar in effect to sexual foreplay. In fact, some experts believe chocolate may be even more effective than foreplay for sexual arousal.

Let's hear it for sex. And chocolate!

And then there's porn

Yes, there is porn. Lots of porn. Tons of porn. All manner of porn. Free porn and paid porn. You can thank the internet for that. There's internet porn of every possible description and every possible position. I have seen porn acts on the internet that I never knew could be done by humans! Today, when it comes to sex, you need no imagination; you can simply access the internet and see it all. Porn is popular. Very popular.

Here are some facts about porn from answers/yahoo.com …

Size of the porn industry $57.0 billion world-wide - $12.0 billion US

Porn revenue is larger than all revenues of all professional football, baseball, and basketball franchises combined.

Average age of first Internet exposure to pornography: 11 years old

Men admitting to accessing porn at work 20%

US adults who regularly visit internet porn sites 40 million

Adults admitting to internet sexual addiction 10%

Breakdown of male/female visitors to porn sites 72% male - 28% female

13% of women admit to accessing porn at work

70% of women keep their cyber activities secret

Are You A Good Lover?

What makes a good lover? Taken from my own extensive and successful experience over many years I can tell you that what makes a good lover is: interest. And passion. If you are interested in sex, and interested in pleasing your partner, a combination of interest, passion and developing lovemaking techniques that work (and work well), will make you a good lover.

There are many books and internet articles that will teach you how to drive your partner wild. You can google "sexual techniques" and add a few to spice up your sex life.

Focus is also important. To be a good lover requires you to totally focus on your partner. This means totally focusing on your partner, not just as a sexual object or a sexual partner but also as a **person**. And focus on them so that nothing else exists in the world; not your worries, not your fears, not your work, not your kids, not your relatives, not your friends, not sports, not shopping, not food or anything else.

When you do all that you make your partner feel special. And feeling special can greatly enhance one's sexuality and sensual enjoyment.

What makes a good lover?
1. interest
2. passion
3. focus
4. technique

Grocery Store Aphrodisiacs

Thanks to dadmag.com and Kevin Nelson here is some interesting information about aphrodisiacs …

"From time to time, every man needs to put a charge in his sex life--particularly if he's married and has children. There's hardly any time for sex, and if he does manage to find some, energy and inspiration are often missing. What he (and most of the rest of us) needs is a good aphrodisiac, something to give that slumbering sex life a rousing wake up call. Sure, you could go halfway around the world and pick up some Spanish fly (which is actually the blister beetle, the ancient's version of Viagra) or rub the milk of a jackass on your penis (another ancient prescription for producing an erection). But there's a much easier way: Make yourself a list and go food shopping.

Sound crazy? Well, the truth is that your corner grocery store is filled with tons of foods and beverages--some well known, some not-that can put you and your partner in the right mood and perhaps even turbo-charge your performance while you're at it. Whether or not you believe that food or drink by themselves can have sexual properties, there's no denying that they can have a certain sensual nature. Good food and sex go together like strawberries and whipped cream. How food smells, how it feels in your mouth, how it feels to the touch, even what it looks like can all stir the sexual juices. So the next time you're shopping for the family, throw a few of these items into the grocery basket for that time when the kids are asleep and you and your partner are at long last alone.

Champagne
Marilyn Monroe's favorite drink … champagne … tops
everyone's list of liquid aphrodisiacs. Light, bubbly,
frivolous and fun, it says to your partner, "Baby, this
is special," and that's a turn-on for her. Champagne in
combination with other foods with sexual associations,
such as strawberries (best served in warm weather,
preferably in bed) or chocolate, is simply irresistible.

As to the type and brand of champagne, that's up to you.
But there is one general rule when seeking to stir the
sexual appetites of women: expensive is better. They like
to feel they're special (which they are), and spending
money on them is a time-honored technique to show that
you think they're special too. The fact that you've gone
to the trouble of arranging something out of the ordinary
shows that you are thinking about them. And remember:
cheap champagne can give you a headache, which pretty
well defeats the purpose, doesn't it?

Chocolate, M& M's (green)
Is there any substance more sinfully appealing to women
than chocolate? Every February the women's magazines
are filled with Valentine's Day articles lauding the
aphrodisiacal qualities of chocolate. Buy the darkest,
most expensive you can find; it's guaranteed to rev up
those pheromones.

A few years ago in Texas, green M&Ms--only the greens,
not the other colors--became known, especially among
teenagers and college students, as a sexual stimulant.
A sorority house in Austin supposedly set aside a jar of

them for "special occasions." For most women, though, even if you separate out the greenies, buying them a bag of M&M's as a prelude to sex probably won't achieve the result you're looking for ...

Strawberries, Grapes, Whipped Cream

Any food that you feed to your partner can potentially fan the flames of sexual excitement. Grapes, the Dionysian fruit of wine, are one. Strawberries--red, juicy, suggestive of warmth and summer--are yet another. Strawberries have the advantage in that you can dip one in whipped cream and feed it to your partner, who may then lick your fingers clean ...

Other Fruits and Vegetables

Juicy and sweet, the tomato was regarded in the 16th century as "the love apple." Its Latin name was pomum amoris and was said to be "so beautiful as to command love." Perhaps a nice tomato soup with potato chip croutons for dinner tonight? No? Well then, how about French onion soup instead? For centuries people have attributed aphrodisiacal qualities to onions. They are fragrant with bell-shaped curving layers inside. According to legend, newlywed couples in France were served onion soup on the morning after their wedding night as a means of restoring their depleted sexual juices.

Some hot-blooded Mediterranean countries believe that hot red peppers stimulate the libido. The ancient Doctrine of Semblances states that any food that looks like a sexual organ may have sexual properties ...

Truffles are also a legendary aphrodisiac, though

definitely not found at your local Ralph's or Safeway. Some specialty stores sell truffle, though, as well as truffle oil. While expensive, a good white truffle oil can add fragrance to various dishes, salads, even french fries.

Seafood
Oysters are one of the best-known aphrodisiacs. Their reputation may be based on their slithery texture and shape. The legendary Casanova ... supposedly ate 50 raw oysters a day. Some men claim good results with lobster. Stay away from the rare Japanese blowfish, though. It's supposed to increase male potency but if the sushi chef doesn't cut it exactly right and you get a bite of fish liver, you die instantly.

Cinnamon Buns, Roast Beef, Pizza
A Chicago neurologist once studied men's responses to smells. He found that men were different than women-- peppermint and chocolate had little effect on their libido. So what did? Turns out that hot cinnamon buns, roast beef, and cheese pizza cause blood to engorge men's penises and make them hard. So after you pick up that pizza tonight, be sure to stop off and get some fresh flowers for her. That way you'll both be happy."

Menu of sex acts

There exists all kinds of sex. Sex is only limited by the imagination (and physical possibility). Here is a partial list of just some of the types of sex that people can, and do, engage in …

Wake up sex
Make up sex
Titty sex
Pity sex
Dress up in a cheerleader or biker costume sex
Talk dirty sex
Phone sex
Boredom sex
Revenge sex
Sexting
Home video sex (often released to the internet)
Rebound sex
SUI (sexing while intoxicated)
Ex-sex (sex with your ex)
Groupie sex (celebrity sex)
Tourist-in-a-foreign-country sex
Presidential sex in the oval office ("oral sex is not sex")
Poison ivy sex (outdoor sex, unknowingly in a poison plant patch)
On the beach sex (sand sex)
In the water sex (wet sex)
Under the water sex (scuba sex)
In the air sex (Mile High Club)
Vacation sex
Honeymoon sex
One night stands

First date sex
Third date sex (mandatory by custom)
Marital sex
Extra-marital sex
Pre-marital sex
Never married sex
Accidental sex (oops, it just "happened")

The list goes on and on.

Sex, Laws and Videotape

When it comes to sex, America is often considered to be prudish, moralistic and puritanical. This probably stems from our history; from when the Puritans settled and controlled New England in the 1600's. Under the Puritans, life was strict, highly regulated, and adultery and wanton sexuality was frowned upon and punished (as in Nathaniel Hawthorne's famous book, The Scarlet Letter).

That era of American history probably later led to a large number of weird laws about sex. In the U.S., in many states, there are quaint, funny and just plain weird laws about sex. Many of these quaint, funny and just plain weird laws about sex are still on the books today.

From Texas A&M University here are some of those weird sex laws ...

A law in Fairbanks, Alaska, does not allow moose to have sex on city streets.

In Ventura County, California, cats and dogs are not allowed to have sex without a permit.

It's safe to make love while parked in Coeur d'Alene, Idaho. Police officers aren't allowed to walk up and knock on the window. Any suspicious officer who thinks that sex is taking place must drive up from behind, honk his horn three times and wait approximately two minutes before getting out of his car to investigate.

Any couple making out inside a vehicle, and accidentally sounding the horn during their lustful act, may be taken to jail according to a Liberty Corner, New Jersey, law.

In Nevada, sex without a condom is considered illegal.

Clinton, Oklahoma, has a law against masturbating while watching two people having sex in a car.

In Willowdale, Oregon, no man may curse while having sex with his wife.

In Harrisburg, Pennsylvania, it is illegal to have sex with a truck driver inside a toll booth.

In Kingsville, Texas, there is a law against two pigs having sex on the city's airport property.

No woman may go in public without wearing a corset in Norfolk, Virginia.

In the state of Washington there is a law against having sex with a virgin under any circumstances (including the wedding night).

The only acceptable sexual position in Washington, D.C., is the missionary-style position. Any other sexual position is considered illegal.

In Connorsville, Wisconsin, no man shall shoot off a gun while his female partner is having a sexual orgasm.

In Bakersfield, California, anyone having intercourse

with Satan must use a condom.

In Oblong, Illinois, it's punishable by law to make love while hunting or fishing on your wedding day.

In Minnesota, it is illegal for any man to have sexual intercourse with a live fish.

No man is allowed to make love to his wife with the smell of garlic, onions, or sardines on his breath in Alexandria, Minnesota. If his wife so requests, law mandates that he must brush his teeth.

Warn your hubby that after lovemaking in Ames, Iowa, he isn't allowed to take more than three gulps of beer while lying in bed with you -- or holding you in his arms.

Bozeman, Montana, has a law that bans all sexual activity between members of the opposite sex in the front yard of a home after sundown if they're nude.

In hotels in Sioux Falls, South Dakota, every room is required to have twin beds. And the beds must always be a minimum of two feet apart when a couple rents a room for only one night. And it's illegal to make love on the floor between the beds!

The owner of every hotel in Hastings, Nebraska, is required to provide each guest with a clean and pressed nightshirt. No couple, even if they are married, may sleep together in the nude. Nor may they have sex unless they are wearing one of these clean, white cotton nightshirts.

An ordinance in Newcastle, Wyoming, specifically bans couples from having sex while standing inside a store's walk-in meat freezer!

In Romboch, Virginia, it is illegal to engage in sexual activity with the lights on.

In Carlsbad, New Mexico, it's legal for couples to have sex in a parked vehicle during their lunch break from work, as long as the car or van has drawn curtains to stop strangers from peeking in.

Women aren't allowed to wear patent-leather shoes in Cleveland, Ohio - a man might see the reflection of something "he oughtn't!"

No woman may have sex with a man while riding in an ambulance within the boundaries of Tremonton, Utah. If caught, the woman can be charged with a sexual misdemeanor and "her name is to be published in the local newspaper." The man isn't charged nor is his name revealed.

It is illegal for any member of the Nevada Legislature to conduct official business wearing a penis costume while the legislature is in session.

Good quotes about sex

There are a number of mechanical devices which increase sexual arousal, particularly in women. Chief among these is the Mercedes-Benz convertible. ~ P.J. O'Rourk

Sex and golf are the two things you can enjoy even if you're not good at them.~ Kevin Costner, Tin Cup

The only thing wrong with being an atheist is that you can't scream "Oh God" during an orgasm. ~ Author Unknown

Nymphomaniac: a woman as obsessed with sex as an average man. ~ Mignon McLaughlin, The Neurotic's Notebook, 1960

Men reach their sexual peak at eighteen. Women reach theirs at thirty-five. Do you get the feeling that God is playing a practical joke? ~ Rita Rudner

When authorities warn you of the sinfulness of sex, there is an important lesson to be learned. Do not have sex with the authorities. ~ Matt Groening

Don't worry, it only seems kinky the first time. ~ Author Unknown

If God had intended us not to masturbate, He would have made our arms shorter. ~ George Carlin

I think I could fall madly in bed with you. ~ Author Unknown

The big difference between sex for money and sex for free is that sex for money usually costs less. ~ Brendan Francis, Playboy

Conservatives say teaching sex education in the public schools will promote promiscuity. With our education system? If we promote promiscuity the same way we promote math or science, they've got nothing to worry about. ~ Beverly Mickins

Sex is one of the nine reasons for reincarnation. The other eight are unimportant. ~ Henry Miller

If we define porn as any message from any communication medium that is intended to arouse sexual excitement, then it is clear that most advertisements are covertly pornographic. ~ Philip Slater quotes

There is nothing wrong with going to bed with someone of your own sex. People should be very free with sex, they should draw the line at goats. ~ Elton John

It's very difficult to fail at porn. ~ Michael Chabon quotes

I love sex. It's free and doesn't require special shoes. ~ (Anonymous)

I read so many bad things about sex that I had to give up reading. ~ Anonymous

Some mornings, it's just not worth chewing through the leather straps. ~ Emo Phillips

Being with a woman all night never hurt no professional baseball player. It's staying up all night looking for a woman that does him in. ~ Casey Stengel

It is not economical to go to bed early to save the candles if the result is twins. ~ Chinese Proverb

Obscenity is whatever gives the Judge an erection. ~ Author Unknown

Is sex dirty? Only if you do it right. ~ Andrew Lawrence

Sex is a huge topic of interest. Billions of people everywhere, all over the world, are interested in, and having, sex. There are thousands of books about sex. There are sex books that deal with the psychology of sex, the physicality of sex, the positions of sex, sexual techniques, books on how to please a man, books how to please a woman and books on how to please yourself. There are thousands of books that cover hundreds of different topics relating to sex.

And then there is Soul Sex. Soul Sex takes sex to a whole new level.

Part 4 Soul Sex

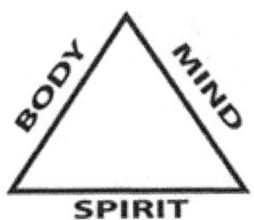

OK, now that you know more about the soul, and sex, it's time for soul sex!

When it comes to sex there are a lot of ways to do it and a lot of different kinds of sex. When it comes to sex, humans can be quite creative. Sex is a natural drive. And depending on one's personality and beliefs and interests there is procreational sex, recreational sex and love sex. Sex can involve one person, two people or more than two people.

The act of sex normally involves the body, and the mind. And the emotions.

Physically and poetically, sex is the union of two people. Emotionally and spiritually, the physical act of sex is often an attempt to "merge", to bring two people as close together as possible, to become "one". Obviously, two people cannot physically merge to become one but the sex act is as close as you can get.

Soul sex is more than sex. Soul sex involves not only the body and the mind but also involves and includes the spirit; the soul. Soul sex is not just the meeting of two bodies, it is the meeting of two **souls**. The meeting of two souls produces spiritual recognition. And spiritual recognition is joyous for the soul. Joyous for both souls who recognize each other, for both souls who meet. Soul sex is not just a meeting of two bodies and two minds it is a meeting of two souls. It elevates sex to a whole new level, a spiritual level. In addition to the physical and mental/emotion dimensions soul sex adds a whole new dimension, a third dimension … the spiritual dimension.

In broad terms spirituality can be religious oriented, non-religious oriented or both.

How spiritual are you?

☐ extremely
☐ very
☐ some
☐ not much
☐ not at all

Soul sex is tied to one's spirituality. The more spiritual you are, the better the soul sex.

Soul sex. How do you do it?

There is no set way to have soul sex. I recommend the following steps ...

1. You and your partner go into a quiet dimly lit room. Candle light is good.
   Make sure there are no distractions for at least 30-45 minutes.

2. Get naked.

3. Sit facing your partner.
   Sit close enough to touch and look into each other's eyes.
   No distractions.
   No talking.

4. Look deeply into your partner's eyes.
   The eyes are the windows to the soul.
   Keep looking deeply.
   Keep looking deeply into each other's eyes until your souls connect (how do you know when your souls connect? You will feel like nodding and/or smiling).
   Do not break eye contact.
   There is no other foreplay allowed. No kissing, no fondling, no caressing.
   You should feel your soul lifting; you should begin to feel love, and joy.

5. Move closer. Keep eye contact. Parts of your body (arms, legs) should now be in contact with your partner's. No penetration yet.

6. Desire builds. The desire to be closer, to meet, to unite, to merge.
   The world no longer exists, there is only you and your partner.
   The desire to unite, to become one, intensifies. It is not simply sexual desire. It also feels like caring, it feels like love, pure caring, pure love. Because it is.

7. When the desire to unite with your partner becomes stronger, and you feel that you must get even closer, you want your souls to connect even more, you want to merge together, totally.
   Get physically closer, let your souls connect even more. Keep looking deeply into each other's eyes.

8. When the feeling to merge with your partner, to become one with your partner becomes unbearable - and you know your partner feels what you feel - then, and only then, do you and your partner physically and sexually join.

   Once joined, do what comes naturally; partners may thrust, hug or do whatever the two souls want to do in order to get as close as humanly possible. As the souls try to merge both you and your partner should feel a unique and spiritual passion, a unique and spiritual passion unlike any either of you has ever experienced

9. Continue until both parties are physically and spiritually satisfied. How do you know? You'll know.

10. Allow yourself and your partner to feel the afterglow

and the deep spiritual joy of your souls having recognized and loved and touched.

This is soul sex. The ultimate pleasure.

There are several other sexual positions which may also work well; missionary, woman on top, side by side. Any position can work as long as both eye contact and penetration can be made and maintained. Feel free to experiment with soul sex and see what works for you and your soul sex partner.

Be sexually responsible. Unless you want a pregnancy, or a sexually transmitted disease, safe sex is always a good idea. Use a condom.

The soul sex example in this book is based on sexual intercourse between a male and a female. Other sexual preferences and practices are known and acknowledged, but as applied to soul sex, are beyond the scope of this book.

Soul sex can be extremely satisfying. If done properly, between spiritually developed partners, soul sex can be completely satisfying. It can satisfy the mind, the body AND the spirit - thus taking sex to a whole new level.

What should you do now? That's up to you.

If it were me, I'd go tend to my soul.

Make the time and take the
time to tend to your soul.
Tend to your soul and you will
enrich your life beyond measure.
Tend to your soul.
Make your soul joyous.
You'll be glad you did!

Andrew

Andrew Lawrence

More enlightenment

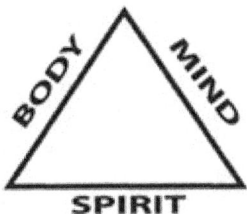

For more enlightenment and inspiration I highly recommend:

- ✔ The Happiness Transformation
- ✔ Discover Your Life Purpose in 30 minutes
- ✔ Stories Of A Lifetime

Free excerpts at Andrew-Lawrence.blogspot.com

Books by Andrew Lawrence

Soul Sex: The Ultimate Pleasure
This book provides fascinating and enlightening insights into the age old mystery of the soul, and introduces a whole new level of sex - soul sex.

The Happiness Transformation
The Happiness Transformation reveals how to be genuinely happy - NOW - and for the rest of your life.

Discover Your Life Purpose in 30 minutes
An interactive book which quickly reveals <u>your</u> unique and special purpose in life.

MONEY - The Basics
An easy to understand book about money. A must-read for anyone who wants to be more money savvy. "The most valuable book you'll ever read".

Stories Of A Lifetime
Inspirational true stories of extraordinary events in an extraordinary life. Amazing and true stories. A motivational masterpiece!

How To Thrive After 65
A little book that reveals the big secrets of a happy retirement. A must-read for every American, age 55 and over.

Free excerpts at: Andrew-Lawrence.blogspot.com